Contents

All the words that appear in **bold** are explained in the glossary on page 30.

Going to school

In the morning Nabia and her mother leave home to walk to Nabia's school.

Nabia's mum takes her to school every day. Nabia is only six years old and is not big enough to go on her own.

4

On My Own

Anne Smith

Photographer: Angus Blackburn

Consultants: The Royal Society for the
Prevention of Accidents

Artist: Roger Fereday

WATCH OUT!

At Home

Near Water

On My Own

On the Road

Editor: Sarah Doughty
Designer: Loraine Hayes

First published in 1991 by
Wayland (Publishers) Ltd
61 Western Road, Hove
East Sussex BN3 1JD, England

© Copyright 1991 Wayland (Publishers) Ltd

British Library Cataloguing in Publication Data
Smith, Anne
On My Own – (Watch out!)
I. Title II. Series
613.6

HARDBACK ISBN 0-7502-0096-0

PAPERBACK ISBN 0-7502-0600-4

Phototypeset by Dorchester Typesetting Group Ltd
Printed and bound by Casterman S.A., Belgium

The road they cross every day is very busy.

To be safe Nabia and her mum have crossed at the **zebra crossing**.

Nabia waves goodbye to her mum at the school gate.

Mum will be there to pick her up in the car when school is over.

WATCH OUT!

At playtime

It is playtime, and Sean has some crisps to eat.

But Fraser is bigger than Sean. He is trying to take Sean's crisps away from him!

Fraser is a **bully** and is teasing Sean.

Fraser takes Sean's crisps. He holds them up high in the air where Sean cannot reach them.

Sean is now very sad. Fraser has eaten all his crisps.

Lindsay asks him what is wrong. She is sorry for Sean and shares her crisps with him.

Mrs Lewis is the teacher on duty in the playground today. Lindsay and Sean go to her. Sean tells her what has happened.

You must always tell a teacher if someone bullies you at school.

WATCH OUT!

Mum is late

When school is over Nabia goes to the school gate.
She finds her mum is not there.

Nabia knows she must not wait at the gate on her
own. She goes back into school.

Mrs Jones is Nabia's teacher. She is still in the classroom after the day's lessons are over.

Nabia tells her that her mother is not at the gate. Mrs Jones says she will phone Nabia's home.

WATCH OUT!

Always tell your teacher if your parent is not there to pick you up from school.

Nabia tells Mrs Jones her telephone number.
Mrs Jones dials the number from the school office.

There is no answer. It could mean that mum is on her way. Nabia watches out for her from the window.

Do you know your own address?
Can you say your telephone number?

While she waits Nabia helps Mrs Jones.

They both tidy up the books in the library.

They are sure that Nabia's mum will soon be here.

Nabia's mum arrives. She is late because the traffic was very busy.

She thanks Mrs Jones for looking after Nabia.

She praises Nabia for remembering what to do when she was late.

WATCH OUT!

Going shopping

Rosie likes to go shopping. She is at the super-market with her mum and sister.

Rosie is busy looking at the shelves. She is trying to see which toy she likes best.

But while she was looking at the toys, her mum and sister moved to another aisle.

Now Rosie cannot see them anywhere.

She stands quite still and looks all around.

WATCH OUT!

If you are lost in a shop you should wait for your parent to come and find you. People who work in shops can also help you.

Kevin works in the supermarket.

He asks Rosie if she needs help.

Rosie knows Kevin can help her. She tells him that she has lost her mother and sister.

Rosie waits with a lady assistant while Kevin speaks over the store microphone.

He tells Rosie's mother to come to the **check-out** counter to find Rosie.

Mum hears Kevin's message. She does what Kevin tells her at once.

Kevin goes with Rosie to find her mum and her sister waiting at the check-out counter.

They are very pleased to see her. Mum says thank you to Kevin.

WATCH OUT!

A visitor calls

The gas man has arrived at Sean's house to read the gas meter.

He checks the address in his book before he rings the front door bell.

Sean and his dad open the front door. The gas man shows dad his **identity card**. Dad looks at the card closely before he lets him in.

Dad is always careful about who he lets indoors.

WATCH OUT!

Dad has a fall

Sean's dad has climbed up a ladder to work on the roof. The ladder is propped against the side of his house.

Sean is going to play in the garden while mum goes to the shops.

The ladder suddenly slips and dad falls down. His leg is hurting him badly.

He calls to Sean to telephone for an **ambulance**.

Sean rings 999 for the **emergency services**. He speaks slowly and clearly on the phone.

He gives his name and address and tells them what has happened.

The ambulance men arrive and strap dad's leg. They will take him to hospital. Dad will soon feel better.

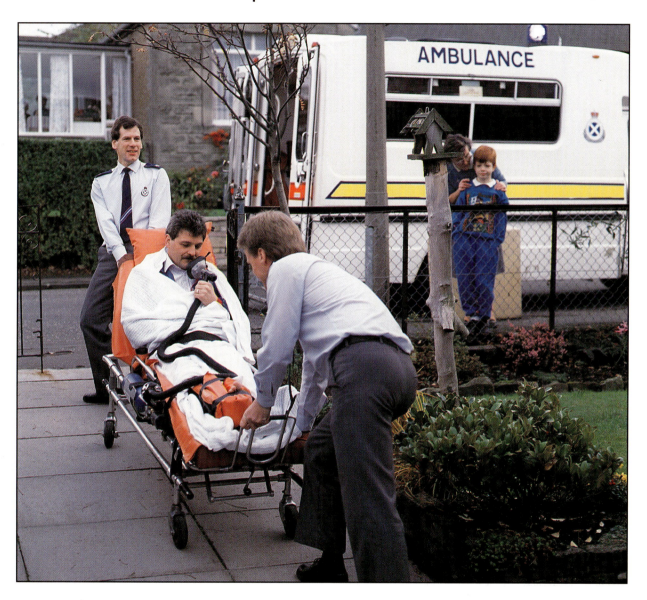

Sean waits with Mrs Thomas who lives next door. Mum will soon be home.

Could you use a public telephone if you needed help? You may be lost, or just want to talk to a friend. At other times you may need to call the emergency services.

If you want to make a call:

1. Find a public phone box.

2. Pick up the receiver and listen for the dialling tone.

3. Put a 10p coin in the slot. (Some phone boxes take special cards which you buy from shops.)

4. Press the buttons carefully to ring the number.

5. Now you will hear the ringing tone. When somebody answers speak slowly and clearly.

Remember that if you want to call the emergency services that the call is FREE.

WATCH OUT!

In the park

Rosie and Karen want to go and play on the swings in the park.

Rosie's mum takes them to the park as they must not go by themselves.

Mum talks to Rosie and Karen as they play together on the swings.

A park is fun to play in but stay with your family and friends. Never wander off by yourself.

WATCH OUT!

Lost in town

Emily has gone into town with her mum and dad.

There were lots of people in the street and Emily got lost.

Luckily Emily saw a policeman and a policewoman. She knew that they would be able to help her.

Emily told them her name and where she last saw her parents. The police will soon have Emily back with her mum and dad.

Glossary

Ambulance A vehicle that carries injured people to hospital.

Bully Someone who is unkind to a person who is smaller or weaker than they are.

Check-out The place where you pay for things you have bought in a supermarket.

Emergency services The ambulance service, the fire brigade, the police force, coastguard and mountain rescue are all emergency services.

Identity card A special card with a photograph which shows who a person is and the organization they have come from.

Zebra crossing A safe place to cross a road if you are careful. There are black and white stripes painted across the road.

Books to read

Come and Tell Me by Helen Holick (Dinosaur, 1986)

Feeling Safe, Feeling Strong by Susan Jerkel and Janic Rerch (Lerner, 1980)

If You Meet a Stranger by Camilla Jessel (Walker Books, 1990)

Taking Care with Strangers by Kate Petty and Lisa Kopper (Franklin Watts, 1988)

We Can Say No! by David Pithers and Sarah Greene (Arrow Books Ltd, 1986)

Notes for parents and teachers

There are many potential dangers facing children today. We have to accept that it is not safe for a young child to be left alone in the house, the shops, in the street or playing in the park.

It is never too soon to prepare a child for when he or she may find themselves in an unsupervised or vulnerable position.

Make sure that your child knows and can say his or her name, address and telephone number. Show your child how to use the telephone at home and at a public call box in case they are lost. Explain how the emergency services can be called in an emergency. Emphasise that 999 is for emergencies only and must never be called at any other time.

Discuss with your child how to recognize people they might ask for help such as teachers, police, road crossing patrol men and women, shop assistants or other adults with children.

Make sure that your child knows exactly who will be meeting him or her from school and where they will meet. Tell your child exactly what to do if no one is there at the meeting place. Let the school know if you think you may be delayed or if someone else is going to collect your child. Set an example by good time-keeping yourself.

When your child is a little older encourage him or her to be independent but insist that he or she tells you where they are going, who they will be with and what time they will be back. Tell your children the same if you go out.

Index